Angular Performance

Optimization

Everything you need to know

Abdelfattah Ragab

Angular Performance Optimization

Everything you need to know

Abdelfattah Ragab

Introduction

Welcome to the book Angular Performance Optimization.

In this book, I will show you all the ways you can optimize the performance of your Angular application. You may already be familiar with concepts like change detection and lazy loading, but there are plenty of other strategies and techniques you can use to significantly improve your app's performance. This book explains these advanced optimization methods and provides you with practical insights and actionable tips.

Whether you are a beginner or an experienced developer, this book is designed to give you the knowledge and tools you need to effectively optimize your Angular applications.

Let us get started.

Why Optimize Angular Applications?

Optimizing Angular applications is crucial for enhancing performance, improving user experience, and ensuring efficient resource management. Key strategies include change detection, lazy loading, and other performance techniques.

How can I measure the Angular Application Performance?

Measuring the performance of Angular applications is essential for identifying bottlenecks and ensuring a smooth user experience. There are several tools and techniques available to help you assess and optimize performance.

Key Performance Metrics
1. **Time to Interactive (TTI):** This metric measures how long it takes for the application to become fully interactive, meaning users can interact with it without delays.
2. **Total Page Load Time:** This measures the overall time taken for the entire page to load, including all resources and dependencies.

Tools for Performance Measurement

1. **Google Chrome DevTools:**
   - The **Performance tab** allows you to record and analyze the performance of your Angular application. You can start profiling while interacting with your app to identify slow areas, particularly during change detection cycles
   - **Lighthouse:** This tool provides automated audits for performance, accessibility, and SEO. It generates a detailed report with actionable insights to help optimize your application.
2. **Angular Augury:**
   This is a Chrome and Firefox extension specifically designed for Angular applications. It helps visualize the application structure and performance, making it easier to identify areas for optimization.
3. **WebPageTest:**
   This tool allows you to test your application's speed from various locations and browsers. It provides insights into loading speed and can help detect performance issues specific to Angular applications.
4. **Protractor:**
   While primarily a testing tool for Angular applications, Protractor can simulate user interactions and help assess performance during end-to-end tests.

Best Practices for Performance Measurement

Profile Regularly: Regular profiling during development can help catch performance issues early. Use the Chrome DevTools to record interactions and analyze the performance data.

Focus on User Interactions: When profiling, interact with the parts of the application that are known to be slow. This targeted approach can yield more relevant insights.

Benchmarking: Establish baseline performance metrics to compare against as you make changes to the application. This helps in understanding the impact of optimizations.

Use Angular Server-Side Rendering (SSR)

Server-Side Rendering (SSR) with Angular Universal is a powerful technique that can significantly improve the performance of your Angular applications. By rendering pages on the server, you can improve initial load times, improve SEO, and provide a better user experience.

Benefits of SSR:

- **Faster Initial Load:** Since the server sends pre-rendered HTML, users can see content faster.

- **Improved SEO:** Search engines can crawl and index your content better if it is rendered on the server, which leads to better visibility in search results.
- **Enhanced User Experience:** Users can interact with the application faster because they do not have to wait for the JavaScript to load and execute before they see the content.

Utilize TrackBy with ngFor

When rendering lists with `ngFor`, Angular can use the trackBy function to recognise which elements have been changed, added or removed. This prevents the entire list from being re-rendered if only a few elements change, which improves performance.

Angular 18 introduces the `@for` syntax, which provides a more intuitive method for traversing elements. This syntax is similar to traditional JavaScript loops.

The @for now forces developers to use a tracking function.

typescript

```typescript
trackById(index: number, item: any): number {
    return item.id; // Return the unique id of the item
  }
```

template

```html
<ul>
```

```
  @for (let item of items; track
trackById) {
    <li>{{ item.name }}</li>
  }
</ul>
```

Change Detection Optimization

Angular uses a change detection mechanism to update the view when the model changes. Angular uses the Default change detection strategy, which checks all components in the component tree. Angular looks for changes to data-bound values in a change detection process that runs after every DOM event: every keystroke, mouse move, timer tick, and server response. To optimize this:

Use OnPush Change Detection: This strategy tells Angular to check for changes only when input properties change or when an event occurs, reducing unnecessary checks.

With the OnPush strategy, Angular only checks the component when:

- An `@Input()` property changes.
- An event occurs within the component.
- An observable linked to the component emits a new value.

This means that if a component's inputs remain the same, Angular skips checking that component, reducing the overall number of checks performed during change detection.

Use Observables and Async Pipe

Take advantage of Angular's reactive programming model by using observables. The asynchronous pipe automatically subscribes to observables and takes care of unsubscribing, reducing memory leaks and improving performance.

To use the `async` pipe, simply bind your observable to the template. Here is an example:

```typescript
import { Component, OnInit } from
'@angular/core';
import { Observable } from 'rxjs';
import { DataService } from
'./data.service';

@Component({
  selector: 'app-data',
  template: `
    <div *ngIf="data$ | async as data;
else loading">
      <ul>
        <li *ngFor="let item of data">{{
item.name }}</li>
```

```
    </ul>
  </div>
  <ng-template
#loading>Loading...</ng-template>
  `

})
export class DataComponent implements
OnInit {
  data$: Observable<any[]>;

  constructor(private dataService:
DataService) {}

  ngOnInit() {
    this.data$ =
this.dataService.getData(); // Returns
an observable
  }
}
```

Use Observables and RxJS Operators to Optimize Data Handling

Optimizing data processing in Angular applications using observables and RxJS operators can significantly improve performance by reducing the number of emissions and managing asynchronous data more efficiently.

RxJS offers a variety of operators that can help you manage data flow and reduce unnecessary emissions. Here are some important operators you should consider:

DebounceTime: This operator delays the output of values from an observable until a certain period of time has elapsed without further output. This is particularly useful for scenarios such as search inputs where you want to wait until the user stops typing before making an API call.

```
import { debounceTime } from
'rxjs/operators';

this.searchInput$
  .pipe(debounceTime(300))
  .subscribe(searchTerm => {
    this.performSearch(searchTerm);
  });
```

DistinctUntilChanged: This operator suppresses duplicate consecutive emissions. It ensures that only unique values are emitted, which can help to reduce the number of unnecessary updates in your application.

```
import { distinctUntilChanged } from
'rxjs/operators';

this.inputValue$
  .pipe(distinctUntilChanged())
  .subscribe(value => {
    this.updateValue(value);
  });
```

ThrottleTime: Similar to debounce, but the first value is output immediately and subsequent values are ignored for a certain duration. This is useful for rate-limiting events such as scrolling or button clicks.

```
import { throttleTime } from
'rxjs/operators';

this.buttonClick$
  .pipe(throttleTime(1000))
  .subscribe(() => {
    this.handleClick();
  });
```

You can use the `pipe` method to link several operators together to create complex data flows while maintaining readability. For example, you can filter, assign and then debounce user input:

```
import { map, filter, debounceTime }
from 'rxjs/operators';

this.userInput$
  .pipe(
    filter(input => input.length > 2),
// Only process inputs longer than 2
characters
    debounceTime(300),
    map(input => input.trim()) // Trim
whitespace
  )
  .subscribe(trimmedInput => {
    this.processInput(trimmedInput);
```

```
});
```

Avoiding Complex Expressions in Angular Templates

Keeping expressions in templates simple is crucial for optimizing performance, particularly during change detection cycles. When complex expressions or function calls are used in templates, they can lead to unnecessary performance overhead, as Angular re-evaluates these expressions frequently.

Why Complex Expressions Are Problematic?

Frequent Re-evaluation: Angular's change detection mechanism runs frequently, especially during user interactions or asynchronous events. If a template contains complex expressions or function calls, Angular will execute these every time change detection is triggered. This can lead to performance degradation, particularly if the expressions involve heavy computations or data manipulations.

Impact on Performance: For example, if you have a function like calculateTotal() in your template, it will be called on every change detection cycle. This means that even if the underlying data hasn't changed, the function will still execute, consuming resources unnecessarily.

This can be particularly detrimental in larger applications where multiple components are involved.

Lack of Change Detection Optimization: Angular cannot determine if the result of a function call has changed without executing the function. This means that even if the input data remains the same, the function will still run, leading to wasted computational resources.

Best Practices for Simplifying Expressions

Use Component Properties: Instead of calling functions directly in the template, compute values in the component class and bind to those properties. For instance, instead of using `{{ calculateTotal() }}`, you can calculate the total in a lifecycle hook (like `ngOnInit`) and store it in a property, then bind to that property in the template: `{{ total }}`.

Utilize Pipes: Angular's built-in pipes can be used to format data without the need for complex expressions. Pipes are optimized for performance and are only re-evaluated when their input changes. For example, using a date pipe to format dates is more efficient than calling a formatting function in the template.

Avoid Function Calls in Templates: In general, you should avoid placing function calls in templates. If you must use a function, make sure it is a simple getter without complex logic. This minimizes the overhead during the change detection cycles.

Leverage Change Detection Strategies: Combining the use of simple expressions with Angular's ChangeDetectionStrategy.OnPush can further improve performance. This strategy allows Angular to skip change detection for components if their inputs do not change, reducing the frequency of checks.

Lazy Loading Modules

By default, NgModules are eagerly loaded. This means that as soon as the application is loaded, all NgModules are also loaded, regardless of whether they are needed immediately or not. For large applications with many routes, consider lazy loading — a design pattern that loads NgModules as needed. Lazy loading helps to keep the initial package sizes smaller, which in turn leads to shorter loading times.

In your app.routes.ts, configure the route to lazy load the feature module using the `loadChildren` syntax:

```
const routes: Routes = [
  {
    path: 'feature',
    loadChildren: () =>
import('./feature/feature.module').then(
m => m.FeatureModule)
  }
];
```

Use the `loadComponent` property to lazy load the standalone component:

```
const routes: Routes = [
  {
    path: 'my-standalone',
    loadComponent: () =>
import('./my-standalone/my-standalone.co
mponent').then(c =>
c.MyStandaloneComponent)
  }
];
```

To improve user experience, you can preload lazy-loaded modules. Import `PreloadAllModules` in your routing configuration:

```
 providers: [
provideRouter(routes,
withPreloading(PreloadAllModules))
]
```

Ahead-of-Time (AOT) Compilation

An Angular application consists mainly of components and their HTML templates. Since the components and templates provided by Angular cannot be directly understood by the browser, Angular applications require a compilation process before they can be executed in a browser.

The Angular AOT compiler (AOT = Ahead-of-Time) converts your Angular HTML and TypeScript code into efficient JavaScript code during the build phase, before the browser downloads and executes this code. Compiling your application during the build process ensures faster rendering in the browser.
Angular AOT compiler is the default starting in Angular 9.

Reduce the Number of API Calls

Optimizing API calls is crucial for improving the performance of Angular applications. Efficient API interactions can significantly reduce load times, improve user experience and minimize resource consumption. Minimizing the number of API requests is crucial. This can be achieved by:

- **Batching Requests:** Combine multiple API calls into a single request when possible. This reduces the overhead of multiple network requests. Use operators such as `forkJoin` to bundle multiple HTTP requests and process them together.
- **Caching Responses:** Implement caching mechanisms to store previously fetched data. This way, you can avoid unnecessary API calls for data that hasn't changed. Using libraries like RxJS's shareReplay can help share the same

observable among multiple subscribers,
preventing duplicate requests

Implement Pagination

For APIs that return large data sets, you should use pagination to limit the amount of data retrieved at once. This not only reduces the initial load time, but also reduces the amount of data processed and rendered in the application at any one time. Other techniques include infinite scroll and virtual scrolling.

Optimize Data Payloads

Ensure that the data sent and received from APIs is as small as possible. This can be done by:
Selecting Only Required Fields: Modify your API to return only the necessary fields instead of the entire dataset.
Using Compression: Enable Gzip compression on your server to reduce the size of the data being transmitted.

Error Handling and Retries

Implement robust error handling for API calls. Use RxJS operators such as `catchError` to handle errors properly and provide fallback mechanisms. Also consider implementing retry logic for failed requests to improve reliability without overloading the server

Debounce User Input

If you make API calls based on user input (e.g. search queries), use debouncing to limit the frequency of requests. This means that the API call is only made when the user has stopped typing for a certain amount of time, reducing the number of calls for quick inputs. Here is an example on how to debounce user input.

```
@Component({
  selector: 'app-search',
  template: `<input type="text"
(keyup)="onSearch($event.target.value)"
placeholder="Search...">`
})
export class SearchComponent implements
OnDestroy {
  private searchSubject = new
Subject<string>();

  constructor(private apiService:
ApiService) {
    this.searchSubject.pipe(
      debounceTime(300), // Wait for
300ms pause in events
      switchMap(searchTerm =>
this.apiService.search(searchTerm)) //
Call the API
    ).subscribe(results => {
      // Handle the results here
    });
  }
```

```
  onSearch(searchTerm: string): void {
    this.searchSubject.next(searchTerm);
// Emit the search term
  }

  ngOnDestroy(): void {
    this.searchSubject.complete(); //
Clean up the subscription
  }
}
```

Use Observables Effectively

Use RxJS Observables to efficiently manage API calls.
Observables can help handle asynchronous data
streams and enable operators that can transform, filter
and combine data streams, making your API
interactions more efficient.

Deferrable Views

Deferrable views are used in the component template to
defer the loading of select dependencies within that
template.
To use this feature, you need to wrap the section of your
template in a @defer block and specify the loading
conditions.

```
@defer {
  <large-component />
```

}
There are many event triggers that you can use, such as on viewport, on timer(5s), when cond, etc..

Utilize Pure Pipes

A pure pipe is a type of pipe in Angular that only re-evaluates its output when the input values change. This means that Angular only re-executes the pipe's transformation logic if the input reference has changed when the same input is passed to a pure pipe multiple times. This behavior is in contrast to impure pipes, which execute their transformation logic on every change detection cycle, regardless of whether the input has changed.

To create a pure pipe in Angular, you can use the `@Pipe` decorator with the default setting (which is `pure: true`). Here's how to implement a simple pure pipe:

```
import { Pipe, PipeTransform } from
'@angular/core';

@Pipe({
  name: 'truncate',
  standalone: true,
  pure: true,
})
export class TruncatePipe implements
PipeTransform {
```

```typescript
  transform(value: string, limit: number = 80): string {
    const trail = '...';
    return value?.length > limit ?
value?.substring(0, limit) + trail :
value;
  }
}
```

```html
<div class="title">{{ product.title |
truncate : 40 }}</div>
```

When using pure pipes, ensure that the input values are immutable or that you create new references when the data changes. For example, if you are filtering an array, make sure to create a new array instead of modifying the existing one.

ngZone

`ngZone` allows you to execute expensive code outside the Angular zone. As long as you are outside the Angular zone, no updates are made to the interface or change detection. Once you have finished executing your code, you can return to the Angular zone to enable change detection.

Use `runOutsideAngular` to run your code outside the Angular zone.

Use `run` to return to the Angular zone.

Optimize Bundle Size

Use the Ivy Compiler: ensure that your application is using the latest version of Angular and that Ivy is enabled in your project.

Lazy Loading Modules: configure your Angular router to load modules on demand

Tree Shaking: tree shaking is a process that removes unused code from your application.

Optimize Third-Party Libraries: Be mindful of the third-party libraries you include in your application.

Minimize Polyfills: Polyfills can add significant size to your bundle. Review your polyfills and remove any that are not necessary for your target browsers. You can also consider using modern JavaScript features that do not require polyfills in modern browsers.

Production Builds: Always build your application for production using the Angular CLI command:

```
ng build --prod
```

This command enables optimizations such as Ahead-of-Time (AOT) compilation, minification, and dead code elimination, which all contribute to a smaller bundle size.

Use a Content Delivery Network (CDN)

Serving your Angular application from a CDN can reduce latency by delivering content from a location closer to the user.

Clean Code Practices

Ensure clean and efficient code by following best practices and coding standards. This not only improves performance, but also makes the application easier to maintain.

Monitor and Fix Memory Leaks

Memory leaks occur when the application releases memory that is no longer required. This can happen for various reasons, such as unhandled subscriptions, event listeners or improperly managed component lifecycles.
To monitor memory usage and identify leaks, you can use Chrome DevTools:

- **Heap Snapshots:** Create heap snapshots to analyze memory usage over time. This allows you to determine which objects are still in memory and whether they should be moved to the garbage collection. You can take a snapshot

before and after certain actions to compare
memory usage.
- **Performance Monitor:** Use the Performance tab
to monitor CPU usage and memory
consumption. Look for spikes in memory usage
that do not decrease over time, indicating
possible leaks.

Common Causes of Memory Leaks

Some frequent culprits of memory leaks in Angular
include:
- **Unsubscribed Observables:** If you do not
unsubscribe from Observables, this can lead to
memory leaks. Always cancel subscriptions with
the ngOnDestroy lifecycle hook or use operators
like takeUntil to effectively manage subscriptions.
- **Event Listeners:** If you add event listeners
directly to DOM elements, make sure that they
are removed when the component is destroyed.
- **Long-lived References:** Keeping references to
components or services that are no longer
needed can prevent garbage collection. Make
sure that you remove references when they are
no longer required.

Fixing Memory Leaks

Unsubscribe from Subscriptions: Always clean up subscriptions in the ngOnDestroy method. For example:

```typescript
import { Component, OnDestroy } from
'@angular/core';
import { Subscription } from 'rxjs';

@Component({
  selector: 'app-example',
  templateUrl:
'./example.component.html',
})
export class ExampleComponent implements
OnDestroy {
  private subscription: Subscription;

  constructor() {
    this.subscription =
someObservable.subscribe(data => {
      // handle data
    });
  }

  ngOnDestroy() {
    this.subscription.unsubscribe(); //
Prevent memory leak
  }
}
```

Use `takeUntil`: This operator can help manage subscriptions automatically:

```
import { Subject } from 'rxjs';
import { takeUntil } from
'rxjs/operators';

export class ExampleComponent implements
OnDestroy {
  private destroy$ = new
Subject<void>();

  constructor() {

someObservable.pipe(takeUntil(this.destr
oy$)).subscribe(data => {
    // handle data
    });
  }

  ngOnDestroy() {
    this.destroy$.next();
    this.destroy$.complete(); // Clean
up
  }
}
```

Check for Detached DOM Elements: Ensure that components are properly destroyed and not left hanging in memory. Use the `ngOnDestroy` lifecycle hook to clean up any references to DOM elements or services.

Optimize Images and Assets

Optimizing images and assets is critical to improving the performance of Angular applications. Here are some effective strategies to achieve this:

Use the `NgOptimizedImage` Directive: Angular offers the directive NgOptimizedImage, which optimizes the loading of images. With this directive, you can effectively manage image loading attributes and ensure that images are only loaded when needed. It also supports features such as lazy loading and responsive images, which can significantly improve performance by reducing the initial load time of your application.

Implement Lazy Loading: Lazy loading images means that images are only loaded when they enter the viewport. This can be achieved with the attribute `loading="lazy"` in your image tags. By deferring the loading of off-screen images, you can improve the initial loading speed of your application.

Optimize Image Formats: Choose the right image formats based on the type of image. For example:
- Use **SVG** for logos and icons, as they are scalable and lightweight.
- Use **JPEG** for photographs, as it provides good quality with smaller file sizes.
- Use **PNG** for images that require transparency.

Additionally, consider using next-gen formats like **WebP**, which offer better compression without sacrificing quality. Implement fallbacks for browsers that do not support these formats.

Compress Images: Before uploading images to your application, use image compression tools to reduce the file size. Tools such as ImageOptim or online services can help remove unnecessary metadata and optimize images without losing quality. Ensure a good balance between image quality and file size to ensure a good user experience.

Use a Content Delivery Network (CDN): Delivering images via a CDN can significantly reduce loading times as the content is delivered from a location closer to the user. Many CDNs also offer built-in image optimization features, such as automatic resizing and format conversion, which can further improve performance.

Preload Critical Images: For images that are critical to the initial rendering of your application (such as hero images), you should use the `rel="preload"` attribute. This will instruct the browser to load these images as quickly as possible, improving the perceived loading speed.

Manage Asset Bundling with Webpack: Angular uses Webpack under the hood to bundle assets. Make sure your assets are properly configured in the `angular.json` file to optimize loading. This includes setting up appropriate paths and making sure images are included in the build process.

Optimizing Videos

Optimizing video in Angular applications is critical to improving performance and providing a smooth user experience. Here are some effective strategies for optimizing video content:

Use Adaptive Bitrate Streaming: Implement adaptive bitrate streaming to deliver video content at different quality levels depending on the user's network conditions. This ensures that users with slower connections receive lower quality streams, while users with faster connections can enjoy higher quality video. Services such as **HLS (HTTP Live Streaming)** or **DASH (Dynamic Adaptive Streaming over HTTP)** can be used for this purpose.

Optimize Video Formats: Formats such as **MP4** (H.264 codec) are widely supported and offer a good balance between quality and file size. Consider using newer formats such as **WebM** or **AV1** for better compression and quality.

Compress Videos: Before uploading videos, use compression tools to reduce the file size without significantly affecting the quality.

Implement Lazy Loading for Videos: Similar to images, "lazy loading" should also be implemented for videos to ensure that they are only loaded when they are to be displayed in the viewport. This can be done with the attribute `loading="lazy"` in the file.

Use a Content Delivery Network (CDN): Make your video content available via a CDN to reduce latency and improve loading times. CDNs cache content in different locations around the world so that users can access videos from a server near them, improving performance.

Preload Important Videos: Use the `preload` attribute in the `<video>` tag to control how videos are loaded. If you set it to `metadata`, only the metadata (such as duration and dimensions) will be loaded without downloading the entire video.

Optimize Video Player Implementation: When implementing a video player in Angular, consider using libraries that provide built-in optimizations and features to improve video playback performance, such as buffer management and responsive design.

Using the <picture> Element for Responsive Images

To optimize your Angular application for different devices, you can use the `<picture>` element to load different images depending on the device's capabilities and screen size. This approach helps improve performance by ensuring that only the most appropriate

image is loaded, reducing bandwidth usage and improving loading times.
The browser selects the most suitable image based on the screen size and capabilities of the device. You can also use the srcset and sizes attributes to provide different image resolutions for different screen sizes. This is particularly useful for responsive designs:

```
<picture>
  <source srcset="image-small.jpg 600w,
image-medium.jpg 1200w, image-large.jpg
1800w" sizes="(max-width: 600px) 100vw,
(max-width: 1200px) 50vw, 33vw"
type="image/jpeg">
  <img src="image-large.jpg"
alt="Description of the image">
</picture>
```

Mobile-First Approach

Start by designing your application for mobile devices first and then gradually improve it for larger screens. This will ensure that the core features are also available on smaller devices, which often have greater limitations in terms of processing power and bandwidth.

Conclusion

Congratulations! You have completed the book "Angular Performance Optimization". Now you will create better Angular applications. Remember that learning Angular is an ongoing process. Practice makes perfect — build your own projects, experiment with the features you learn, and delve into the extensive online resources.

Thank you for joining me in my exploration of Angular. I wish you the best of luck on your programming journey. Have fun programming and good luck with your applications!

Media Attributions

Modern annual report magazine page flyer a company catalog
Image by starline on Freepik

Clock and increasing chart. Workflow productivity increase, work performance optimization, efficiency indicator. Rising effectiveness metrics. Vector isolated concept metaphor illustration
Image by vectorjuice on Freepik

Don't miss out!

Receive an email when Abdelfattah Ragab publishes a new book. It's free and without obligation.

Also by Abdelfattah Ragab

Shippo is a multi-carrier shipping solution designed to streamline the shipping process for businesses of all sizes.
By integrating shipping into your application, you can create better types of e-commerce applications.
You will learn how to create the labels, calculate shipping costs, and get the fastest, cheapest, and best rates.

By the end of the book, you will be able to enable shipping in your Angular application and handle all kinds of scenarios.

Stripe is a leading payment processing platform that enables businesses to accept online payments.
By integrating payment processing into your application, you can create all kinds of e-commerce applications.
You will learn how to create the checkout session, how to use webhooks events and finally how to go live.

By the end of the book, you will be able to process payments in your Angular application and handle all kinds of scenarios.

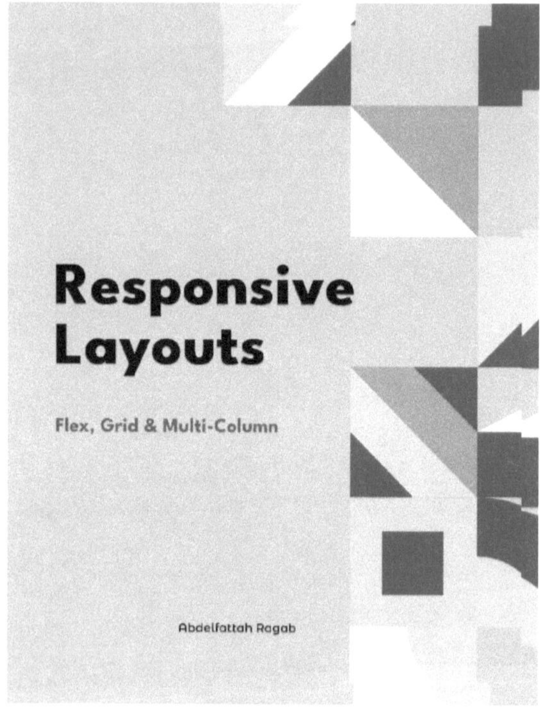

Responsive design is an approach to web design that ensures web pages render well on a variety of devices and screen sizes, from desktop monitors to mobile phones. The primary goal of responsive design is to provide an optimal viewing experience, making it easy for users to read and navigate the site with minimal resizing, panning, and scrolling.

In **"Angular Portfolio App Development"** you will learn how to create an online portfolio app to showcase your skills to the world and your potential employers.

Angular Shopping Store

From Scratch to Successful Payment

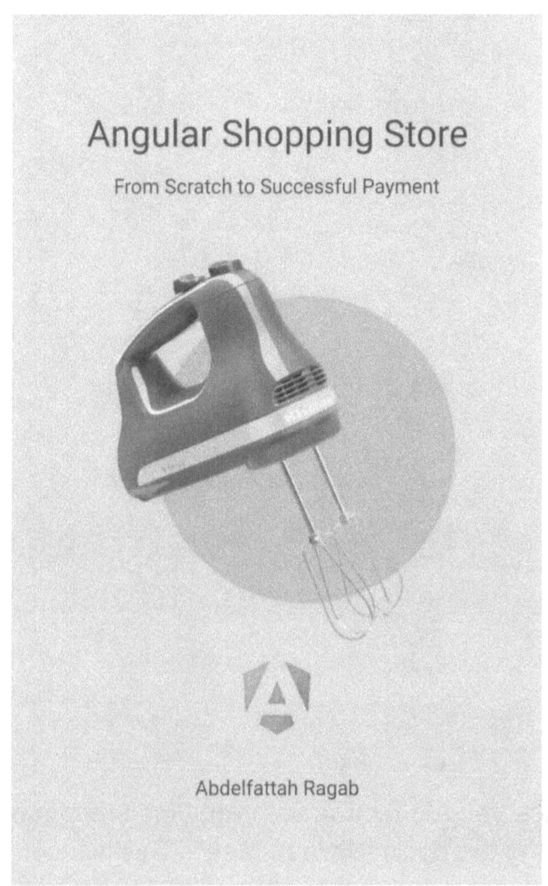

Abdelfattah Ragab

In **"Angular Shopping Store"** you will learn how to create a simple Angular ecommerce store. It's a good introduction to the world of full-stack development.

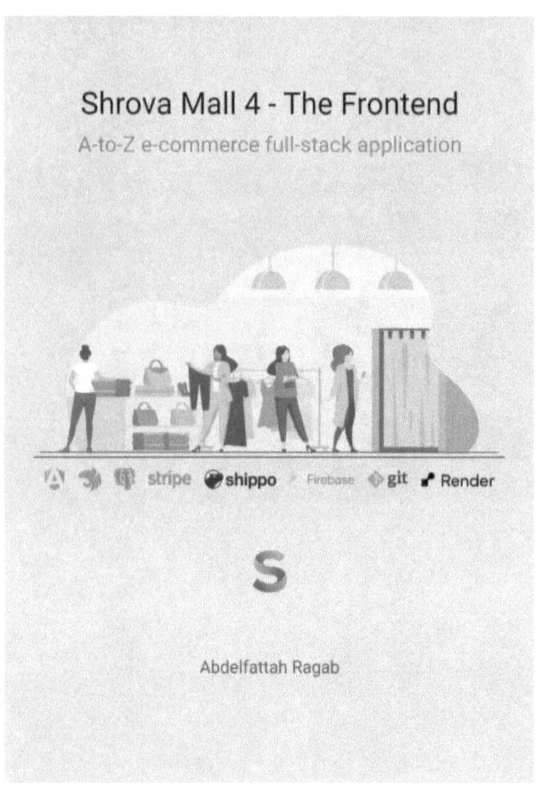

Once you are familiar with Angular, I recommend reading the book **"Shrova Mall"**. This is a complete e-commerce solution that allows you to ship products to customers and accept payments online, among other things. It is a professional full-stack project where you will learn a lot of things.

About the Author

Abdelfattah Ragab is a professional software developer with more than 20 years of experience.
https://abdelfattah-ragab.com

About the Publisher

Abdelfattah Ragab is a highly qualified and experienced software developer with over 20 years of experience in the industry. Specializing in front-end development, Abdelfattah Ragab has a deep understanding of Angular, JavaScript, TypeScript, HTML and CSS. Read more at https://abdelfattah-ragab.com

www.ingramcontent.com/pod-product-compliance
Lightning Source LLC
LaVergne TN
LVHW041802190726
843493LV00008B/2745